REAL ESTATE WEALTH CREATOR

WORKBOOK

Hello Real Estate Wealth Creator,

Welcome! I'm thrilled you're here.

This workbook isn't just another set of exercises — it's your **implementation guide** to begin living the real estate wealth-building life you were meant for. Whether you're new to real estate or finally ready to take consistent action, you are in the right place.

In Chapter 5 of the companion book, I share the value of Getting Started. Here's the truth: **momentum is your secret weapon**. Don't wait for perfection. Those who succeed are the ones who act, reflect, adjust, and keep going.

If you haven't yet taken the Real Estate Investor Assessment, that's your first move. Take 5 minutes now to get your personalized starting point:

REI Assessment

Throughout this workbook, you'll find guided prompts, exercises, and action steps to turn insight into implementation. **You won't just think like an investor — you'll become one.**

Let's create your real estate dreams, one intentional step at a time.

CHAPTER ONE

CULTIVATING THE RIGHT MINDSET FOR WEALTH CREATION

Wealth starts within. It doesn't begin with a property or a large bank account — it begins with your definition of wealth and the mindset you cultivate to help you reach your wealthy place.

Most people never stop to define what wealth truly means to them. But you will. Because wealth demands clarity.

AS YOU REFLECT, YOU'LL NOTICE SOMETHING: THIS LIFESTYLE COMES WITH A COST. THAT'S WHERE REAL ESTATE COMES IN — AS A PROVEN VEHICLE TO HELP FUND YOUR WEALTHY LIFE.

WEALTHY LIFE REFLECTION QUESTIONS

What kind of work gives me purpose?

How do I want to provide for my loved ones?

What does excellent health look like for me?

Where do I envision living?

What amount of money would I like to earn?

What causes do I want to support?

What legacy do I want to leave behind?

INNER GAME CHECK-IN

What negative beliefs about money or wealth might be holding me back?

What empowering beliefs do I already have that support my financial growth?

What new beliefs am I ready to adopt on my wealth journey?

ACTION STEP SUMMARY

WRITE YOUR PERSONAL DEFINITION OF WEALTH.

DESCRIBE YOUR IDEAL WEALTHY LIFE USING AT LEAST THREE QUESTIONS ABOVE.

IDENTIFY ONE LIMITING BELIEF TO RELEASE AND ONE EMPOWERING BELIEF TO STRENGTHEN.

COACH'S CORNER

You just laid your foundation. This clarity will become your compass. Keep this vision front and center. You're building something real, and it starts here.

CHAPTER TWO

THE ROLE OF FAITH IN REAL ESTATE WEALTH CREATION

Real estate and faith aren't opposites. In fact, they belong together.

From Genesis to Revelation, real estate is everywhere in scripture. God gave land to His people. He instructed stewardship. He multiplied through ownership.

When you embrace real estate as a spiritual and practical calling, you begin to see it as a means to serve, grow, and fulfill purpose.

FAITH & REAL ESTATE REFLECTION QUESTIONS

Do I believe real estate aligns with God's plan for my life?

What Scriptures stood out to me from Chapter 2?

How does seeing God as a landowner shift my mindset?

What verse or affirmation keeps me inspired?

How can I use real estate to uplift my community?

ACTION STEP SUMMARY

Choose a Scripture or affirmation to anchor your wealth vision.

Journal how your faith supports your investing journey.

Identify one way to use real estate to bless others.

COACH'S CORNER

Faith is your foundation. Real estate is your tool. Keep them aligned, and you'll build wealth with meaning, purpose, and peace.

CHAPTER THREE

RAISING YOUR FINANCIAL INTELLIGENCE

The wealthiest investors aren't just rich in assets. They're rich in **financial intelligence**.

In Chapter 3, we explored the 8 characteristics of financially literate people. Now it's time to assess where you're strong and where you're ready to grow.

FINANCIAL IQ CHECK-IN

Which of the 8 traits do I currently demonstrate?

Which traits do I want to develop this year?

How do I view debt: as a danger or a strategic tool?

FINANCIAL LITERACY ISN'T ABOUT PERFECTION. IT'S ABOUT *PROGRESS*.

ACTION STEP SUMMARY

Write down your top 2 strengths from the 8 characteristics.

Choose one financial area to improve in the next 30 days.

Reflect on how your perspective on debt may be evolving.

COACH'S CORNER

Money isn't mysterious. It's a game with rules you are learning to master. Keep showing up. The more literate and intelligent you become, the more powerfully you can act.

CHAPTER FOUR

THE FOUR REAL ESTATE WEALTH GENERATORS

There are four main ways real estate creates wealth:

1. **CASHFLOW**
2. **APPRECIATION**
3. **TAX BENEFITS**
4. **DEBT PAYDOWN**

Understanding these gives you vision and clarity about how real estate works for you.

WEALTH STRATEGY REFLECTION QUESTIONS

Which wealth generator excites me most? Why?

What are my thoughts about house hacking or landlording?

How might I begin experimenting with one of these strategies?

ACTION STEP SUMMARY

Choose your favorite wealth generator and journal why.

Research one real estate strategy that aligns with your goals.

Write down any initial fears you have about being a landlord or investor.

COACH'S CORNER

You're not just learning. You're building a real wealth plan. These four tools are your building blocks. Learn them. Use them. Prosper through them.

CHAPTER FIVE

GETTING STARTED AS A REAL ESTATE WEALTH CREATOR

Starting can be the hardest part. But it doesn't have to be.

This chapter helps you uncover your "Big Why" and explore what might be holding you back. Clarity leads to courage.

START STRONG REFLECTION QUESTIONS

- What are my personal goals for investing?
- What's my "Big Why"?
- Which of the 4 Pillars of Getting Started spoke to me most?
- What obstacles or disempowering beliefs are in my way?

ACTION STEP SUMMARY

Write your top 3 goals for investing in real estate.

Describe your "Big Why" in 1-2 sentences.

Identify one mindset shift you need to make to get started.

COACH'S CORNER

You're ready. Starting isn't about having it all figured out. It's about moving with intention. Take one step today—the next one will get easier.

CHAPTER SIX

BUILDING YOUR REAL ESTATE TEAM

No one builds wealth alone. Your **team** is your secret weapon.

Start with your Starting 5 (agent, lender, contractor, property manager, lawyer), and then grow from there.

TEAM BUILDER REFLECTION QUESTIONS

- Who is already on my real estate team?

- Who do I need to add?

- How can I organize my team using the FFM Formula (Find, Fund, Monetize)?

- What strategy do I want to master first? What's next?

ACTION STEP SUMMARY

Make a list of your current team members.

Identify 1-2 key relationships to build.

Choose on monetization strategy to start with.

COACH'S CORNER

Your dream team is out there. As you grow, attract recruit partners who share your values and vision. **Remember you are only as good as your team.**

CHAPTER SEVEN

TIME FOR ACTION

Now it's go time.

This final chapter invites you to choose **what to act on now**, identify any hesitations, and look for collaboration opportunities.

ACTION REFLECTION QUESTIONS

Which of the 7 action steps am I ready to take?

Which one gives me pause?

What collaborations or partnerships could jumpstart my progress?

ACTION STEP SUMMARY

Choose one action step to complete this week.

List one person you could partner or brainstorm with.

Reflect on any remaining resistance and how to move through it.

COACH'S CORNER

You've done the work. Now, do the work. Small steps compound. Stay consistent. And remember: **wealth favors the action-taker**.

REAL ESTATE RULES OF THUMB

(QUICK REFERENCE)

Use these as tools to quickly analyze deals:

- **70% Rule:** Max purchase price = ARV x 70% - Repairs
- **1% Rule:** Monthly rent should equal 1% of the purchase price
- **GRM:** Price ÷ Gross Annual Rent
- **50% Rule:** Estimate half of rent will go to expenses (not mortgage)
- **Cap Rate:** NOI ÷ Purchase Price
- **RTV:** Monthly Rent ÷ Purchase Price (aim for 0.8%-1%+)

Use these as guides, not absolutes. Consider everything through the lens of your market, goals, and objectives.

www.ingramcontent.com/pod-product-compliance
Lightning Source LLC
LaVergne TN
LVHW070901210926
848482LV00016B/988